THE UNTOLD TRUTH ABOUT ALCOHOL:

Understanding why you are addicted and your journey to successful recovery(sober).

Clara walker

Table of contents

Chapter 1

Liquor as a medication

Liquor: Is It A Drug
Indeed, liquor is a medication. In particular, liquor is a Psychotropic Central Nervous System (CNS) Depressant. Being a Psychotropic medication implies liquor affects insight, feelings, and discernment. Liquor imparts this assignment to numerous other notable medications, like Marijuana, Cocaine, and LSD. Being a CNS Depressant implies that liquor eases back the movement of the cerebrum; it likewise

shares this characteristic with numerous different medications like Ambien, Xanax, and Valium.

A piece of the explanation some erroneously don't believe liquor to be medication is a direct result of how standardized the utilization of liquor is. Another explanation is a direct result of the way the expression "medications and liquor" has entered the dictionary; the expression misleadingly suggests that liquor isn't itself a medication. Some specific vested parties have even campaigned for supplanting the expression "medications and liquor" with "liquor and different medications" so that it's GABA, or gamma-aminobutyric clear that liquor has a place in the last class.

Chapter 2

Liquor as a toxin

For some's purposes, it very well may be difficult to understand that liquor is a poisonous synthetic. Without a doubt, it can make a party more exuberant and it can draw out the social side of individuals, but at what cost? The body is seriously impacted by the proceeded utilization of liquor, and the overall population should know this. There are two poisons in liquor that the body needs to endeavor to dispense. These are acetaldehyde and acidic corrosive.

Acetaldehyde is a vapid fluid made by oxidizing ethanol.

What's more, liquor is a dull, combustible fluid that comes in different structures. Notwithstanding, the structure that is utilized in drinks like wine, lager, and alcohol is known as ethyl liquor. It is delivered through the maturation of grains and organic products, which happens when yeast follows up on specific fixings in food and makes liquor. Lager and wine are drinks that are matured and can contain somewhere in the range of 2% to 20% liquor. Furthermore, different beverages that are refined, like alcohol, can contain somewhere in the range of 40% to half of the liquor.

Regardless of the sort of cocktail, in any case, liquor is risky to the body. The liver does most of the difficult work in handling liquor and eliminating it from our framework. Nonetheless, around 10% of liquor is additionally disposed of through our breath, sweat, and pee. Anything that remains in the body will gradually be dispensed with throughout the following 7-12 hours following drinking. Albeit the liver accomplishes the hardest work in taking out poisons, liquor use influences the wide range of various significant organs too. The head researcher of a concentrate on liquor addiction detailed the accompanying: "Obviously liquor misuse can think twice about design and usefulness of a few human organs, in this way straightforwardly expanding the gamble of death," The review referenced here likewise uncovered that heavy drinkers might be more in danger for specific sorts of malignant growths. This review and other examination investigations have discovered that liquor abuse can add to the accompanying medical issues:

Hypertension
Unpredictable heartbeat
Barrenness
Unpredictable feminine cycles
Pancreatitis

Stroke

Disarray

Amnesia

Cirrhosis

Dementia

Seizures

Gout

Hypertension

Nerve harm

Night sweats

Besides, customary utilization of liquor can add to glucose prejudice as well as stoutness, which are both connected to Type II diabetes. It ought to be noticed that most nations have a rule for liquor use for people, For example, as per the National Institute of Alcohol Abuse, men ought to try not to drink something like 4 beverages in a day or something like 14 beverages each week. Ladies ought to try not to drink something like 3 beverages in a day or something like 7 beverages each week.

In any case, these rules are established to limit the harm that liquor as of now has on individuals' wellbeing and prosperity. It's implied that liquor additionally adds to wrongdoing, destructive fender benders, and different types of substance use. It can likewise assume a part in self-destruction endeavors and one's general mental wellbeing. On the off chance that you or somebody you know is consistently drinking liquor, consider the above well-being gambles. If you believe you want to support in finishing your drinking, contact a psychological well-being supplier quickly.

Chapter 3

Medical advantages of Alcohol

7 Health Benefits Of Drinking Alcohol

Getting squandered consistently probably won't be ideal for your physical or mental prosperity, yet moderate liquor utilization might have some significant medical advantages. It ought to be noticed that liquor utilization and its advantages fluctuate in light of a singular's body cosmetics and type.

As per the Dietary Guidelines for Americans, "moderate liquor utilization is characterized as having dependent upon one beverage each day for ladies and up to two beverages for men. This definition is alluding to the sum consumed on any single day and isn't expected as a normal more than a few days."
Presently, we've all heard the justifications for why liquor is awful for you, however, what might be said about the advantages? Here is our rundown of seven different ways that savoring liquor control (when you're of the lawful drinking time obviously) could help your wellbeing.

1. It Can Lower Your Risk Of Cardiovascular Disease

The School of Public Health at Harvard University viewed that "moderate measures of liquor raise levels of high-thickness lipoprotein, HDL, or 'great' cholesterol, and higher HDL levels are related with more noteworthy security against coronary illness. Moderate liquor utilization has additionally been connected with helpful changes going from better aversion to insulin to enhancements in factors that impact blood clotting...Such changes would generally forestall the development of little blood clumps that can hinder conduits in the heart, neck, and mind, a definitive reason for some coronary failures and the most widely recognized sort of stroke." This finding applies to all kinds of people who have not been recently determined to have any sort of cardiovascular sickness.

2. It Can Lengthen Your Life

Drinking at times could add a couple of years to your life. A concentrate by the Catholic University of Campobasso detailed that drinking under four or two beverages each day for people individually could diminish the gamble of death by 18%, as revealed by Reuters. "Little sums, ideally during dinners, this has all the earmarks of being the correct method for drinking (liquor)," said Dr. Giovanni de Gaetano of Catholic University, one more creator of the review. "This is one more element of the Mediterranean eating routine, where liquor, a wine most importantly, is the best accomplice of a supper or lunch, yet that's it in a nutshell: the remainder of the day should be without liquor."

3. It Can Improve Your Libido
In opposition to earlier convictions, fresher exploration has found that moderate drinking could against erectile brokenness similarly that drinking red wine could help coronary illness. In a recent report

distributed in the Journal of Sexual Medicine, specialists observed that the possibility of erectile brokenness was decreased by 25 to 30 percent among liquor consumers. The lead specialist, Kew-Kim Chew, a disease transmission expert at the University of West Australia, led the review with 1,770 Australian men. In his review, Chew warily noticed that he and his group, not the slightest bit are encouraging men to stir things up around town and that further exploration is expected to associate weakness and liquor utilization precisely.

4. It Helps Prevent Against the Common Cold

The Department of Psychology at Carnegie Mellon University found that while weakness to the normal virus was expanded by smoking, moderate liquor utilization prompted a decline in like manner cold cases for nonsmokers. This study was directed in 1993 with 391 grown-ups. In 2002, as per the New York Times, Spanish scientists found that by drinking eight to 14 glasses of wine each week, especially red wine, one could see a 60-percent decrease in the gamble of fostering a virus. The researchers thought that this had something to do with the cell reinforcement properties of wine.

5. It Can Decrease the Chances Of Developing Dementia

In a review that included more than 365,000 members beginning around 1977, as detailed in the diary Neuropsychiatric Disease and Treatment, moderate consumers were 23% less inclined to foster mental impedance or Alzheimer's sickness and different types of dementia. "Modest quantities of liquor may make synapses more fit. Liquor in moderate sums stresses cells and consequently hardens them up to adapt to significant anxieties not too far off that could cause dementia," said Edward J. Neafsey, Ph.D., co-creator of the review, as announced by Science Daily. "We don't suggest that nondrinkers begin drinking," Neafsey said. "However, moderate drinking — assuming it is moderate — can be gainful."

6. It Can Reduce The Risk Of Gallstones
Drinking two units of liquor each day can decrease the gamble of gallstones by 33%, as per scientists at the University of East Anglia. The investigation discovered that the people who detailed polishing off two UK units of liquor each day had a 33% decrease in their gamble of creating gallstones. "Specialists accentuated that their discoveries show the advantages of moderate liquor admission however stress that over-the-top liquor admission can cause medical conditions," as indicated by the review.

7. Brings down The Chance Of Diabetes
Consequences of a Dutch report showed that solid grown-ups who drink one to two glasses each day have a diminished

possibility of creating type 2 diabetes, in contrast with the people who don't drink by any stretch of the imagination. "The consequences of the examination demonstrate the way that moderate liquor utilization can have an impact in a solid way of life to assist with lessening the gamble of creating diabetes type 2," specialists said in an explanation to Reuters.

Chapter 4

Liquor consequences for the mind and fixation

However liquor is viewed as socially OK to polish off in many regions of the planet, weighty liquor use can demonstrate impeding to an individual's physical and mental prosperity and the general physiological soundness of their cerebrum. Weighty or long-haul liquor use can bring about learning and memory issues and can likewise at last lead to the turn of events or compounding of emotional wellness conditions.

The mind is a fragile and multifaceted organ that should keep a cautious equilibrium of synthetic substances, called synapses, for an individual to appropriately work. Liquor inebriation can upset this fine equilibrium, upsetting the cerebrum's normal harmony and long haul, persistent use powers an individual's mind to adjust with an end goal to make up for the impacts of liquor.

Maybe one of the most disturbing long-haul impacts of liquor use on the cerebrum is the possible improvement of physiological reliance, a state, and condition where an individual encounters physical and mental withdrawal side effects and desires on the off chance that they stop drinking or fundamentally bring down how much liquor in their body.

An individual who is reliant upon liquor is in danger of fostering an AUD, a cerebrum sickness portrayed by a battle to restrict drinking, regardless of critical pessimistic impacts on somebody's very own wellbeing, connections, and by and large friendly working.

While a portion of liquor's physical and mental impacts blur once somebody quits drinking, others might endure for longer timeframes and have long-haul wellbeing outcomes.

Transient Effects of Alcohol on the Brain

Liquor inebriation is a consequence of momentary impacts on the focal sensory system with side effects that can differ radically contingent upon how frequently somebody drinks, how much liquor they polish off, their interesting substantial cosmetics, and their weight. Side effects of liquor inebriation, like gentle mental and actual hindrance, may become obvious after only 1 or 2 beverages, yet heavier use can bring about a liquor glut assuming that somebody ingests a lot of liquor during one sitting.

The quick impacts of liquor on the cerebrum are because of its effect on the organ's correspondence and data handling pathways. Tragically, drinking too vigorously or too quickly can bring about a few unfriendly mental impacts, like disarray, hindered engine coordination, and declined thinking skills. Keeping on drinking regardless of perceiving indications of this can prompt a liquor glut, now and again alluded to as "liquor harming".

Liquor harming is a hazardous and possibly lethal outcome of drinking a lot of liquor in a short measure of time. Liquor-harming side effects might include:

Disarray.

Seizure.

Issues with staying cognizant.
Respiratory concealment.
Pulse easing back.
Spewing.
Super durable mental disturbance or disability.
In the most pessimistic scenarios, passing.
Long haul Effects of Alcohol on the Brain
The people who drink all the more intensely are at expanded risk for unfriendly liquor-related entanglements, particularly if they drink unreasonably over significant periods. Long-term wellbeing dangers of persistent liquor use incorporate heart, liver, and absorption issues, malignant growth, safe framework debilitating as well as state of mind and rest aggravations, and the advancement of other emotional wellness issues, including wretchedness and nervousness.

Liquor can cause enduring mischief for your mind and result in shrinkage of the organ area known as the hippocampus. In one concentrate by the University of Oxford, specialists followed members for quite some time, following their drinking examples and mental wellbeing. Members in the review who drank or more beverages daily had very nearly multiple times the gamble of hippocampus shrinkage contrasted with nondrinkers.

The people who use liquor exorbitantly and for extensive periods likewise risk thiamine lack because of unfortunate sustenance, which might bring about the advancement of Wernicke-Korsakoff Syndrome (WKS), now and again usually alluded to as "wet cerebrum". This condition can create enduring mental turmoil, eye development aggravations, trouble with coordination, and relentless learning and memory issues.

Ultimately, long-haul liquor misuse can likewise prompt the advancement of a liquor use jumble (AUD), which may in some cases be alluded to as having a "liquor fixation" or "liquor addiction".

An AUD is an impulsive, risky example of liquor utilization that continues regardless of pessimistic outcomes to an individual's wellbeing, position, and individual connections. For an emotional wellness expert to determine somebody has an AUD, an individual should meet no less than two of the accompanying rules inside a year span:10

Investing a lot of energy attempting to get liquor.

Encountering desires for liquor.

Drinking while in circumstances where it's perilous to do such, for example, while driving or working hardware.

Proceeding to drink regardless of familial and relationship issues brought about by liquor use.

Being not able to satisfy commitments at work, home, or school due to liquor use.

Utilizing higher or more incessant measures of liquor than initially expected.

Resistance, or requiring higher measures of liquor to accomplish past impacts.

Being not able to eliminate drinking.

Proceeding to drink despite negative physical or emotional wellness results.

Keep away from exercises that you once appreciated so you can drink.

Encountering liquor withdrawal side effects assuming you attempt to quit drinking.

Download our pamphlet to get more familiar with our methodology, treatment contributions, and recovery offices.

Liquor Consumption in the U.S.

Liquor is viewed as socially OK in the United States, and numerous Americans polish off liquor consistently. Drinking excessively, in any case, can be destructive to your wellbeing. Between the long periods of 2011 and 2015, liquor misuse was answerable for around 95,000 passings, and unnecessary liquor utilization likewise caused the demise of 1 of every 10 grown-ups between the ages of 20 and 64.3

The 2018 National Survey on Drug Use and Health reports that 139.8 million Americans matured 12 or more established presently drink liquor, 67.1 million were viewed as gorge consumers in the previous month, and 16.6 million were delegated, weighty drinkers.11

The NIAAA characterizes hard-core boozing as polishing off sufficient liquor to raise your BAC to 0.08 g/dl in a solitary event. This by and large means 4 beverages for ladies and 5 for men inside a time of around 2 hours. 2 Binge drinking can prompt the improvement of an AUD, and in 2018, 14.1 million grown-ups ages 18 and more established were accounted for to have an AUD.

What Effect could Alcohol at any point Have on my Mental Health?

Individuals might encounter worked-on friendly communication or general sensations of prosperity with moderate liquor utilization. In any case, it's essential to comprehend that liquor use can represent a gamble on somebody's psychological well-being, general temperament, and everyday mental working because of its effect on mind synthetic compounds. Liquor use - particularly exorbitant liquor use - can compound previous comorbid mental issues, like sadness and tension. In others, liquor might actuate misery and uneasiness. Mental impacts of liquor use might incorporate cognitive decline, issues with learning, dementia, and seriously prevented mental working in most extreme cases. Looking for liquor compulsion treatment is the most important phase in forestalling or decreasing the adverse consequences of liquor on the cerebrum.

It's never past the time to turn your life around, regardless of how critical your circumstance might feel at the time. Connect for help today and get the consideration you want. By looking for compulsion treatment, you can reclaim your life and forestall or lessen a large number of the dangers related to liquor misuse.

Chapter 5

Recuperation from Alcohol habit and the excursion to a more joyful and satisfying life

Recuperating from liquor addiction is certainly not a direct or simple interaction. Generally, a few types of expert assistance and treatment is required.
While the cycle for a recuperating alcoholic is without a doubt testing, it is conceivable and especially beneficial. In many instances

of liquor habit, recuperation is lifesaving and important to endurance.

Recuperation from liquor addiction - The recuperation cycle in 8 basic advances

From dynamic liquor abuse to everyday sober living, there are various moves toward the course of recuperation. These means should be taken for the best long-haul result.

The means might appear to be straightforward in themselves however we don't misjudge the mental fortitude and responsibility it takes to make everyone.

Stage 1 of recuperating from liquor addiction - Asking for the right assistance. It is critical to request the right assistance. A specialist, somebody in recuperation from liquor addiction, a liquor guide, or one of our Delamere liquor specialists can help prompt and back you in getting to liquor recuperation.

Stage 2 of recuperating from liquor addiction - Stopping liquor securely. If you are a liquor subordinate, you should go through a liquor detox to guarantee you stop liquor securely. At Delamere we put your security and solace first, giving a full clinical liquor detox directed every minute of every day by our group of specialists, guides, and qualified nursing staff.

Stage 3 of recuperating from liquor abuse - Resolving and mending the justifications for why you drank. When you have securely quit drinking the justifications for why you drank must be thoroughly tended to. This will assist you with bettering and comprehending yourself and help with forestalling backslide. Injury and private matters ought to be treated by a certified specialist/guide. Emotional well-being diseases will likewise be thoroughly treated by a specialist and specialist.

Stage 4 of recuperating from liquor addiction - Learning new methods for dealing with stress and recuperation conduct.

To abstain from returning to your old way of dealing with especially difficult times of drinking and broken ways of behaving, it is fundamental to learn new and strong survival strategies. These methods can be learned through mental social treatments. Certain all-encompassing treatments are likewise demonstrated to help the recuperating and recuperation process.

Stage 5 of recuperating from liquor abuse - Implementing change into your life and idiot-proofing your recuperation against backsliding. Learning the devices of recuperation is a certain something, carrying out them under tension is very another. You will commit errors. However long you give your all to correct them and see your recuperation from liquor addiction as an expectation to learn and adapt, you will go on in your self-awareness.

Stage 6 of recuperating from liquor abuse - Ensuring you have the right help to assist you with keeping up with alcoholic recuperation and keep on developing. Your old drinking companions will be of no utilization to you getting level-headed. As a recuperating alcoholic, it is essential to have the right continuous assistance and backing, to get to an enticement-free climate. This might be through going to AA gatherings, seeing a liquor advocate, or going to rebuild aftercare.

Stage 7 of recuperating from liquor addiction - Continue to practice and utilize the devices of recuperation. There is no enchanted pill with regards to recuperating from liquor fixation. It requires investment, persistence, constancy, and eagerness to constantly adjust and advance. If you keep on placing the devices of recuperation into down-to-earth application consistently you will receive every one of the rewards alcoholic recuperation brings to the table.
Liquor abuse is an ongoing backsliding cerebrum illness and is moderate. To defeat your useless relationship with liquor, there

is quite a lot more required than simply halting drinking.

A heavy drinker mind will in any case see liquor as an answer for issues and sentiments UNLESS you are resolved to change and open to learning new ways of dealing with hardship or stress.

Recuperating and change frequently require proficient treatment, guidance, and progressing support. Every one of the sentiments that have been stifled by liquor will rise to the top when you at long last figure out how to stop. For this reason, it is crucial to manage these feelings, considerations, and sentiments in a demonstrated and safe manner.

Many recuperating drunkards need continuous help until the end of their lives to remain sober. There is no disgrace in requiring support, your recuperation will constantly have to start things out.

Consistently, a great many Americans effectively complete ongoing treatment for drug or potentially liquor habits. For some, the possibility of restoration can be startling as it implies confronting evil spirits, working through psychological weight, and gaining solidarity to avoid impacts that might prompt a backslide. Returning to a sound and cheerful way of life is difficult, yet with steadiness and a couple of objectives, it's feasible.

Be that as it may, revamping your life after dependence doesn't need to be an overwhelming encounter. While there will without a doubt be days that current difficulties, collectedness, at last, makes the way for the existence of joy.

The following are 10 different ways you can carry on with a blissful and solid existence in recuperation!

Eat a Healthy Diet

Despite becoming abstinent from liquor or potentially tranquilizers, your body has likely been missing legitimate supplements for a significant time. For this reason, a fair eating routine is essential to the recuperation interaction. Not exclusively will it decidedly affect your temperament and conduct, but it can likewise assist with remaking harmed tissues and organs. Keep away from sugar, refined carbs, and caffeine. Eat cancer prevention agent-rich food sources and make certain to top off on fiber and excellent lean proteins.

Stay with a Sleep Schedule

No confidentiality there's a critical connection between dependence and rest. People battling with substance use are 5 to multiple times bound to have rest problems. Since compulsion is additionally known to upset your body's circadian rhythms, predictable, quality rest is vital to keeping up with recuperation.

Begin an Exercise Routine

Figuring out consistently can assist with reestablishing your mind's equilibrium of "inspirational" endorphins known as dopamine. Also, exercise can assist with controlling desires, decrease pressure, and further develop energy levels. In the beginning, phases, begin slow and move gradually up. The way to get into the progression of a workout routine is to find exercises you appreciate. Attempt a thoughtful yoga class or take standard strolls to get some daylight and natural air.

Learn Stress Management Techniques

In the beginning phases of recuperation, it's vital to have pressure executives plan to set up to assist with forestalling the chance of backsliding. One of the most incredible assets for backslide counteraction is an abbreviation called HALT, which represents Hungry, Angry, Lonely, or Tired. At the point when these essential requirements are not met, it's substantially more prone to go to foolish ways of behaving instead of sound survival strategies.

Be More Mindful

Habit frequently remains inseparable from sensations of culpability and disgrace. In any case, rehearsing care in recuperation can assist with quieting pessimistic identity questions. To put it plainly, care is the act of concentrating completely on the current second, paying heed to what you're thinking or potentially feeling, and eliminating channels, judgment, and analysis from your viewpoints. In time, and with committed practice, care can revamp a dependent cerebrum by training it in new and better ways of answering pressure, desires, and triggers.

Put forth Goals (and Work to Keep Them)

Objective setting is a crucial instrument in the recuperation tool compartment. Besides the fact that objectives give a feeling of motivation throughout everyday life, they can likewise cause your excursion to appear to be less scary. Begin by characterizing an all-encompassing long-haul objective. From that point, make more modest momentary objectives that follow the S.M.A.R.T system - - explicit, quantifiable, feasible, practical, and ideal.

Practice Self Love

At first, liquor or potentially medications can cause individuals to feel more certain, vivacious, and loaded with life. As a general rule, in any case, these sentiments are simply a deception, a cover for the well-established close-to-home aggravation and weaknesses that an individual is so frantically attempting to escape. To remain blissful and solid in collectedness, being tenacious about rehearsing confidence is significant. Make positive day-to-day confirmations. Begin journaling. Peruse uplifting books. Furthermore, in particular, indulge yourself with sympathy and thoughtfulness.

Encircle Yourself with Positive People

Falling once more into your old, poisonous group is a dependable method for imperiling your temperance. This isn't to imply that you ought to just spend time with level-headed individuals. Try to encircle yourself with individuals who support your wellbeing and empower your prosperity by considering you responsible for your activities.

Investigate New Hobbies
One of the many delights of collectedness is having newly discovered spare opportunities to find new leisure activities and interests. Filling your timetable with positive exercises that advance solid mental or actual excitement is particularly significant in the beginning phases of recuperation. Why? Since a lot of spare energy can prompt one of the most widely recognized backslide triggers: fatigue. Begin by conceptualizing and making a rundown of every movement that strikes a chord. You may be astounded

to figure out what truly arouses your curiosity!

Offer in return
In dynamic enslavement, losing a viewpoint on the things that matter in life is simple. Recuperation opens up the entryway for new encounters and associations - - sans substances. An extraordinary method for expanding bliss and energy is through chipping in. Not exclusively will you end up working on your self-assurance, you can likewise bring a feeling of significance and reason back to your life and others.

Alcohol Is not the answer, it makes you forget the question.